# SCHIRMER'S LIBRARY
## OF MUSICAL CLASSIC

# F. MAZAS

Op. 36

# Forty Selected Studies

## For the Violin

Critically Revised by

SAM FRANKO

**IN TWO BOOKS**

Book I — Library Vol. 1258

Book II — Library Vol. 1259

# G. SCHIRMER, Inc.

DISTRIBUTED BY

HAL•LEONARD®
CORPORATION

7777 W. BLUEMOUND RD. P.O. BOX 13819 MILWAUKEE, WI 53213

# Forty Selected Studies
## BOOK II

## XXI
### The Staccato

F. Mazas. Op. 36
Revised by Sam Franko

Allegro moderato

# XXII

## Staccato

Allegro moderato

# XXIII

## The Martellato

Firm stroke from middle to point
Allegro moderato

# XXIV
## Bowing Exercise over Two Strings
For flexibility of the wrist

Allegro
leggiero

## XXV

### Bowing Exercise

**Musette**
Andantino

dim. poco ritard.                                    Tempo I°

# XXVI
## Bowing Exercise

Allegro moderato

# XXVII
## Bowing Exercise

This study may also be played with the following bowing:

At the point, with as little bow as possible

Allegro

# XXVIII

## Bowing Exercise

The eighth-notes well accented, with broad strokes at the point

**Allegro non troppo**

# XXIX

## Trill-Exercise

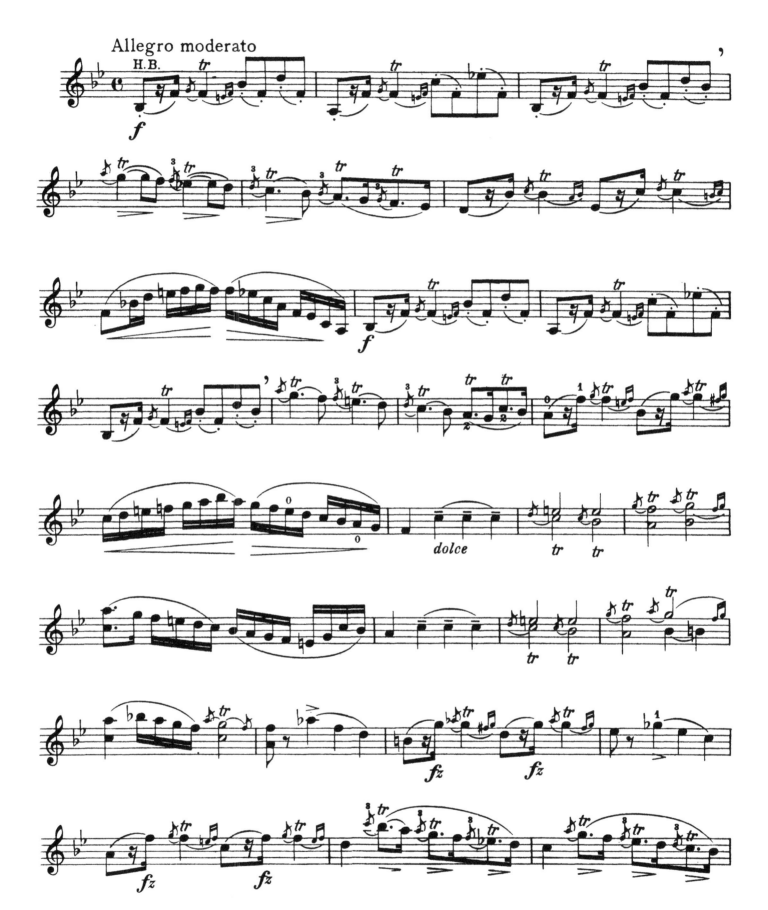

# XXX
## Mordent-Exercise

# XXXI

## Finger-Exercise

Allegro moderato

# XXXII
## Finger-Exercise

**Allegro leggiero**

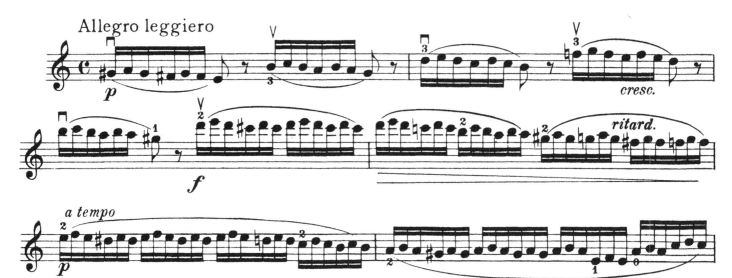

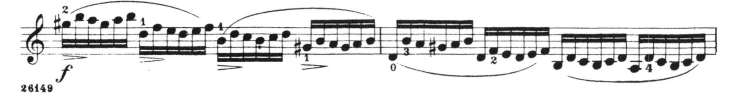

Tempo I⁰

## XXXIII

### Melody on the G-string

Andante sostenuto

# XXXIV

## Finger-Exercise

D.C.

# XXXV
## A Series of Arpeggio-Studies

It is advisable to practise this preparatory exercise before taking up the Study. For chord practise:

After practising this study slowly at the middle of the bow (détaché– – –) accenting each of the bass notes, play the same study with springing bow (spiccato · · ·). Then play two notes in each bow (spiccato) as is marked below.

### Allegro

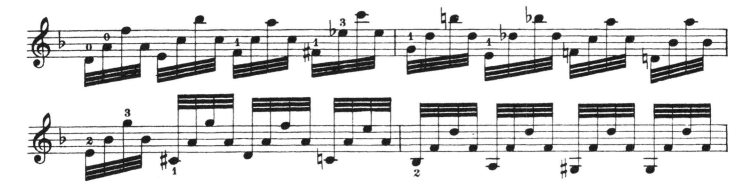

# XXXVI

The preceding exercise with three notes in one bow, instead of two.

# XXXVII

## Slurred Arpeggios

It is advisable to practise this preparatory exercise before taking up the Study.   For chord practise:

*) Keep the 1st, 2d and 3d fingers down

26149

# XXXVIII
## Three-note Arpeggios over Four Strings

For chord practise

It is advisable to practise this preparatory exercise before taking up the Study.

Allegro

segue

# XXXIX

## Arpeggio over Four Strings

# XL

## Arpeggios over Four Strings

Maestoso sostenuto

Allegretto

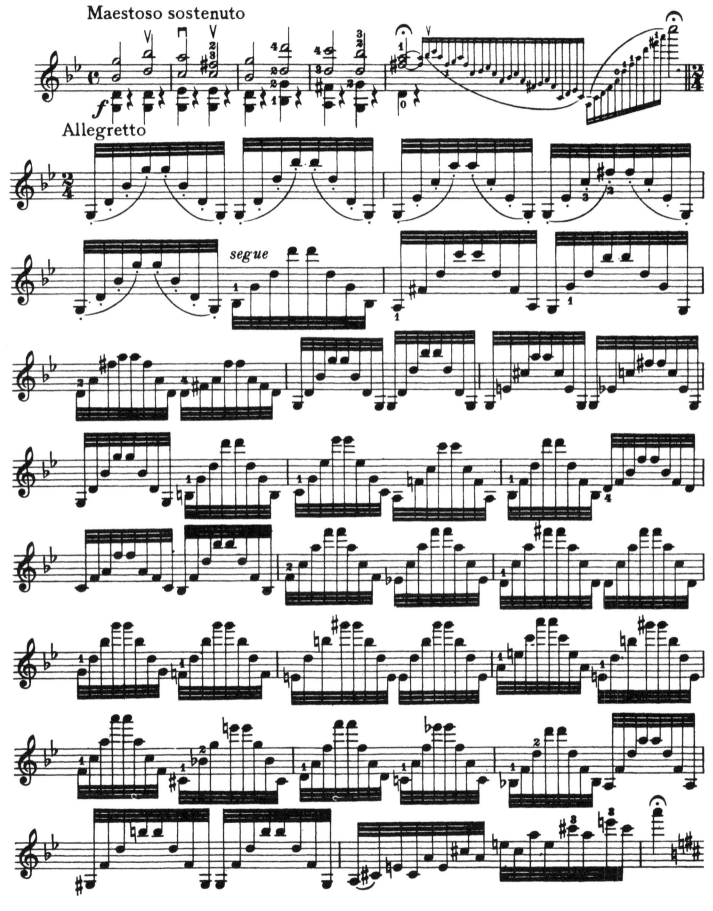

segue

*) Keep all fingers down

26149